Table of Contents

Introduction:

When you think about retirement, what comes to mind? For some, it is Bermuda shorts and a sandy beach. For others, it may be miles of green turf driving in a golf cart. For me, it would be backpacking across Europe with my wife and exploring shops and cafes. If you work hard, any of these scenarios can be yours.

Retirement can be whatever you want it to be, or it can be stress and a lack of finances. Your outcome all depends on your planning. In this book, I will go over some tips on how to attain a more idealistic retirement. Let me help you avoid some financial stress that plagues millions of Americans. Together, we'll discuss how you can make a plan. Through proper and methodical research, this book will assist you in building a formidable plan that accommodates all your retirement needs.

Let's get started.

Chapter 1: Building a Solid Foundation

Financial Independence the Smart Way

Day in and day out you have worked hard. Waking early every morning to make it to the office by 9am and being the best, you can be. Now, you're starting to see more of your time in the office in your rearview mirror and, you're wondering to yourself, *what's next?* Well, even if you have already been putting money aside, it's time to start forming a detailed plan.

The key is to set a goal, perhaps retirement by age 70, and determine what milestones you must hit to get there. An integral part of this is learning how much you must have saved to meet this goal. Consider what you've already put away if you've put anything way, and ask yourself how much is left.

Now, how will we get that money? If you choose to do it the way I'm suggesting, it's through thoughtful and logical investments.

Types of Investments

There are three types of investments that I will discuss in this book. They are **cash reserves, bonds, and common stocks.**

Cash Reserves are short-term investments where an investor deposits some cash and receives a return in 3 months or less. They provide relatively low yields which rise or decline in accordance with short-term interest rates. Some types of cash reserves include bank deposits and money market funds. With cash reserves, you can expect little to no fluctuation in the value of the money deposited. They may not have a huge return, but for the risk-averse, these are generally risk-free investments.

Bonds are interest-bearing obligations issued by the government and corporate bodies. They provide a higher yield than cash reserves, but the interest you pay fluctuates as dictated by market conditions. Bonds can either be corporate or government. Bonds have a guaranteed return; you get your money paid back at a specific date in addition to interest on the loan. Another lower risk option.

Stocks are pieces of a corporation that an investor can buy and assume a part-ownership of that corporation. They can provide the highest yield when compared to both cash reserves and bonds, but also assume the highest risk. As a stockholder in a corporation, you are entitled to dividend payouts from that corporation. The value of dividends fluctuates depending on the performance of the company. You can buy and sell stocks on the stock exchange.

I will go more deeply into these as we progress, but for now this introduction will be enough to provide you with a fundamental understanding of your options. These are three solid options that I recommend, but be sure to speak with your financial advisor to determine what's best for you.

Five Basic Rules of Investing

1. **Learn, Learn, Learn**

   The world of investments can be intimidating, but if you are willing to take the time to learn you can do well. Dedicate time to learn the mechanisms of the financial markets and how it fluctuates. Don't invest your hard-earned money without first learning everything there is to know about that investment. As Benjamin Frankly said, "an investment in knowledge always pays the best interest." My hope for you is that this book is a great starting place on your journey to learn all it is you need to know to guarantee a successful retirement.

2. **Consistency Is Key**

Consistency is important when investing. You should find out a working strategy and stick to it. Do not let your actions be swayed by the waves of emotions or market fluctuations that you cannot avoid. One common practice among investors is what is known as **"market timing."** This is when investors attempt to sell their stocks when the prices are high and repurchase when they are low. Do not fall for it or you will be more likely to fail. Skepticism is an important weapon in investment and financial planning. Do you want to be a successful investor? Of course. Never succumb easily to the breezy words of the market "geniuses," and the seeming omniscience of market pundits. Keep an open mind, but don't sway too easily. If you've made a point of following the first rule and learning what you need to know, then trust your gut and be consistent!

3. Be Balanced

The risk is scary. Period. I do not recommend you go all in like it's the end of the night at the blackjack table. However, on the contrary, I do not recommend not taking any risk and reaping minimal reward. My suggestion is to find a happy medium. What is that perfect balance? Unfortunately, I can't tell you exactly what is right for you. That happy balance depends on factors such as the age of the investor, the investor's responsibilities, and their goals. But if you've learned all there is to know and are ready to remain consistent with your plan; I trust you'll find the right balance for you.

4. **Diversify Your Portfolio**

As you read over the types of investments in the previous section, did any one stand out? Great! I'm glad you're starting to connect with the material. Now I'm going to tell you something you may like less, that one type of investment won't be enough. You must diversify your portfolio to avoid the saying of "putting all of your eggs in one basket." What you'll come to learn is that different investments will react contrarily to the same economic event. What leads to a plummet in stock prices may cause a rise in the value of your bonds. Inversely, stocks will perform well when a country is experiencing economic growth; the reverse is the case for bonds. Diversifying reduces the chance of your entire portfolio being wiped out by a single event. What a diversified portfolio does for you is to help offset losses that are incurred in other investments.

5. **Be Cost Conscious**

When you set out incurring lots of costs on your investments, you inevitably reduce your return on those investments. The wise investors know which risks to take and when to take them. The prudent investor must be conscious of the cost of their investments. To be successful, you must be both. You know what your limitations are and you know your goal for retirement, keep both figures in mind when making your investments. You can do this!

Forming a Strategy and Avoiding Pitfalls

Still with me? Good. I'm glad to hear it. Now you've learned three types of investments and five basic rules to guide you on your journey to become a successful investor. If you're truly determined to reach your retirement goal – whatever that means for you – follow these rules diligently and they will guide you towards that vision.

It's strategy time. Your strategy ensures you have a target, a vision, and a methodical plan to get there. Investing without a strategy leaves you vulnerable to pitfalls like market timing or fluctuations in the market. A solid investment strategy is **dollar cost averaging**. This is a practice in investments that involves investing a fixed dollar amount on a regular schedule regardless of fluctuations in the market. In the case of mutual funds, this can be implemented by using electronic transfers from your personal accounts. Dollar cost averaging is good for people looking to minimize risk, and it helps avoid emotional investing. It is a logical thing to implement a long-term strategy. If you are short on time, this strategy may not work for you.

When forming your strategy, it is important to avoid common mistakes investors make that may sound like good ideas but should be avoided. At the top of my list is buying the most recent best performer. It may seem like an obvious winning strategy, perhaps even wise, but history has repeatedly told us this is not a good idea. These stocks are shooting stars, and they shine for only so long. Don't get stuck with a laggard.

Let's take the things we've learned here, do our research, follow the rules, and get that strategy together. You can do it! But there is still more to learn, so let's continue.

Allocate Your Assets

What do I mean by allocate your assets? I'm referring to distributing the right amount of your time and money into both long and short-term planning through stocks, bonds, and cash reserves. By this point I hope you've learned, these should all be present in your retirement portfolio. How much of your investment should be in equities and how much should you put in fixed income? These are questions that **asset allocation** will answer.

It's time to allocate, or divide, your assets (savings) among your cash reserves, bonds, and stocks. The right way to do this is based on four personal factors.

1. Financial situation
2. Objectives
3. Time horizon
4. Ability to tolerate risk

These factors will vary based on who is forming their plan and allocating their assets. Which one is the most important? In my opinion, it is time. Time will influence all three others. Short on time? You'll have to be willing to take on a lower risk to ensure you don't have to worry about losing cash you need. Your time will also influence your objectives because your goals will be limited by how long you have. You won't be able to change your financial situation, but you will have to find a way to make it work.

For a retirement plan, you generally want to look for investments that have the best long-term potential, but don't forget that you also have short-term needs.

Long-Term Planning: Consider commitments of five years or longer. Stocks offer the best growth potential in the long run, but are fizzling investments over a short period. Stay consistent in these investments and be cost conscious for your greatest return. Your long-term investments are your end game. These are the ones you rely on for college savings for your kids and retirement savings for yourself.

Take a moment to think about what you'll need. **How much money will you need to cover that?** Answering that will help you determine how much to invest in this plan. Consider your potential return when making these investments and be willing to let it accumulate at a slower pace. Your best long-term investment: stocks.

Short-Term Planning: These are commitments you'll need in the next five years. It's important to have short-term investments in case of an emergency. Herein lies another example of why it's important to keep your portfolio diversified. These short-term investments help with things such as saving for a car, a "rainy-day fund," or going on a vacation. Essentially, they are things you'll need cash for within the next five years.

Take a moment to think about what you'll need. **How much money will you need to cover that?** Answering that will help you determine how much to invest in this plan. Consider your potential return when making these investments and be willing to let it accumulate at a slower pace. Your best short-term investment: bonds and cash reserves.

Bonds are great considerations for your short-term plan. As we discussed, they'll preserve your capital but offer a lower return. Dividing your assets amongst these investment categories is important. How you retire and the kind of life you get to live as a senior citizen greatly depends on these strategic choices. Your investment plan should lay great emphasis on growth. The best time to start is now. Whether you're in your 20s, 30s, or 60s, there isn't a better time than the present. You have a time horizon extending to decades. I intend to assist you in making every second count.

Chapter 2: The Stock Market

Bear Markets

Everyone who invests in the stock markets sets out to make money and get a reasonable return on their investment. Many investors achieve these goals, but they wouldn't be able to without strategy and precision. As we've covered in Chapter 1, the risk is high. Stocks are volatile. However, if you are consistent, the risks of common stocks are reduced. When you invest in equities, you are taking a risk, but this risk can be mitigated by thinking long-term.

Be smart with your investing!

At least once in a lifetime of every investor, they are bound to experience a prolonged period of falling prices – sorry, I don't make the rules. This is what people call a "bear market." There isn't a definitive standard as to how steep the dive in prices should be before it's called a bear market, but any drop of at least 20% is generally accepted. Long-term investors wait out the storm and turn out to be the winners. They also take advantage of the lower prices during a bear market to add to their portfolios.

Set Reasonable Expectations

Expectations on return should be reasonable. When a short-term investment is made returns tend to be unpredictable, even when they are over a term of several years. Expectations should be guided by long-term historical averages. History is one of the greatest teachers of the financial world.

How do you draw inferences from historical events? Three major components are necessary for forecasting returns from common stocks: **the dividend yield, the rate of growth in earnings, and the impact on total return from changes in the initial price-earnings multiple for stocks.**

Stock Market Strategies

As we previously covered, you need a strategy when investing. This is especially true when you invest in the stock market. Ignore the people who get steady and reasonable returns on their investments by winging it. They are the exception, not the rule. Adopt a strategy that works and be consistent!

Two strategies to explore are **growth investing** and **value investing**. A **growth investor** focuses on companies with strong earnings and high revenue potentials to get above-average prospect for capital growth with less emphasis on dividend income. If you don't mind volatility with the hopes of a greater increase in share price, growth investment is for you. A **value investor** is attracted to companies based on their assets and earning history. Shareholders usually get paid dividend incomes by these companies. If you want dividend income and potential for capital gain, value investing is for you. Being a growth or value investor depends on the risk that you as an investor is willing to take and your tolerance for short price fluctuations.

Market approaches

The strategy you have mapped out to approach the market depends on the results of your market analysis. As we covered in the basic rules: learn, learn, learn! Investors should never dive into the market without conducting a careful analysis. Market approaches are broken up into analytical strategies. I'll go into detail on a few of those.

Fundamental Analysis

The fundamental analysis is primarily concerned with value. It examines factors in the market that determine a company's expected future earnings and dividends. When these factors are considered, an attempt is made to put a value on the company's stocks. The fundamentalist then seeks out stocks that are trading below their perceived values with the notion that the stock market will eventually discover the real value of these stocks and their price will increase accordingly.

Technical Analysis

Technical analysis is primarily concerned with the history of a stock to predict its future value. This is based on the idea that the stock market follows a discernible pattern and if that pattern can be identified, the balance of the pattern can be predicted and utilized to yield good returns. However, many academic studies have concluded that the technical analysis approach is very unlikely to succeed.

The Buy-And-Hold the Market Approach

The Buy-And-Hold the Market Approach is a benchmark used to measure other approaches to the market. This approach provides returns that would be obtained by buying and holding the stock market. This approach is used as a benchmark because none of the other approaches based on analysis are valid unless they can outperform the market over the long-run.

Buying on margin

Buying on margin is only used if you feel confident and optimistic about a stock that you're willing to take an additional risk on to receive a possible increase in your return. Conversely, when you purchase a stock, and you get that stifling feeling a stock is about to drop in price, you sell short. If your feelings about the stock turn out right and it does drop in price, then you're in a good position to make a profit. If you are wrong about the stock, it may be hard to tell the extent of your losses as the value could keep rising indefinitely. This strategy contradicts one of the basic rules of being consistent but could work if you're willing to assume heightened risk.

Dividend Reinvestment Plan

When approaching the market, you can also consider the cost of a dividend reinvestment plan, also known as DRIP. DRIP refers to reinvesting the dividends you receive from a company into the purchase of more stocks, essentially increasing your investment in the company. DRIPs are always lower in cost compared to buying stocks through a broker. The only costs you might encounter in a DRIP are service charges and prorated brokerage. There are no special tax advantages to this plan, and when your dividends are reinvested, the IRS considers that taxable amount to be equal to the fair market value of the shares acquired with the reinvested dividends. This is a good long-term investment plan because you accumulate additional shares of stock. It effectively provides an easy to implement dollar-cost-averaging plan.

Effects of Transaction Costs

Weigh these market approaches to determine which suits you best. Take into the account the effect of transaction costs when comparing strategies. There are three important factors here you must consider when investing in stocks. They are commissions, the bid-ask spread, and taxes.

Commissions: These are the costs of selling and buying shares of stock and are typically two to five percent of your investment.

The Bid-Ask Spread: This is the difference between the price at which a stock can be bought and the price at which it can be sold. An actively traded stock will have a narrower spread than a stock that is thinly traded.

Taxes: You enjoyed the profit on the sale of your stock, but now you must pay taxes on that profit. You can defer these taxes by holding onto the shares. If you do that you'll continue to earn a return, but ultimately it will be a liability, and you'll still have to pay the taxes on your earnings.

Chapter 3: Risk Management and Investments

Dollar Cost Averaging

Dollar cost averaging, as we previously discussed, is a low-risk strategy that allows you to benefit from the ups and downs of the market. You invest the same amount of money at regular intervals over an extended period. Being that you plan to ride it out, it ultimately makes less of a difference what the mood of the market was when you began. Whether you're just beginning or have experience with stocks, this is one of the simplest and most effective ways of building your investment portfolio. It should only be used for long-term investments. This is not a recommended short-term strategy.

Indexing

When an investor attempts to replicate the investment returns of a stock or bond market index, this is known as **Indexing**. Indexing is a passive approach to investing that emphasizes broad diversification and low portfolio trading activity. One of the primary appeals to indexing is that it is relatively inexpensive. Indexing eliminates the urge of selecting individual funds based on past performance that inevitably reverts to the average of all funds. It is appealing is to long-term investors who

seek a very competitive investment return through broadly
diversified portfolios.

Investment Sectors

When seeking long-term growth and avoiding undue risk,
investment in stocks of quality and established companies seem
to make a lot of sense. A wise investor should focus his research
on a quality company that has fallen out of favor with investors
and invest when the fundamentals and price are right.

If you're in search of an aggressive approach to capital growth,
an **investment in science and technology** may just be the right
decision for you. However, you must be ready to accept the
above average price fluctuations securities in this category are
likely to experience.

Investing in financial services stocks and mutual funds have
proven very profitable to investors in recent years. The sector
has broadly outperformed broad market ranges and hasn't
suffered as much as many others in market corrections.

There is an investment strategy knows as the **"dogs of the dow"
strategy**. You implement it by purchasing the ten highest
yielding stocks in the Dow Jones Industrial average holding
them for twelve months and then rebalancing the portfolio to
take in any new high yielders. You're simply selling stocks that
are no longer in the top ten and buying any that are new to the
list. This strategy is just as simple as it sounds.

There are benefits that an investor could enjoy from **investing
in bond mutual funds**. Some of these benefits include

diversification, active management, low cost, liquidity and no maturity date. When selecting a bond mutual fund, an investor must follow these four steps; establish your time horizon, keep credit risks in mind, gauge your tolerance for interest rate risks, and consider investment costs.

Investing in US treasury securities is easy and very profitable. You can invest in these securities by setting up a treasury direct account without paying any commissions, fees or other charges. This account links to your savings or checking account.

A good choice for an investor who is out to manage and minimize risks would be **investing in real estate investment trusts**. A REIT is an organization that specializes in the ownership of an income-producing real estate or related loans or interests. Equity REITs invest most of their assets directly in real property and derive their income primarily from rents.

Mortgage REITs invest in loans on real estate property. REITs combine elements of real estate and stocks provide investors a practical and efficient means to professionally manage real estate in their portfolio.

If you already have a well-rounded portfolio of domestic securities, it is advisable you turn your eyes towards **international investments**. They offer you a participation in the growing economies beyond the shores of the United States, additional diversification, and potentially high rewards.

Emerging markets are another platform that offers you diversification of your investment portfolio. Emerging markets present much higher risks to investors in comparison to developed stock markets. What they offer is a potential for capital gains. However, an emerging market fund may represent an attractive opportunity for a small portion of your portfolio.

Investment Strategies: "The Bucket Approach"

I will attempt to address three investment strategies that we will call 'buckets.' These buckets are divided based on income, relative safety, and growth.

Bucket 1 (The Income Bucket)

This is a strategy that considers less risky investments that generate income while allowing the other buckets to grow. Some individuals with potentially long-life expectancies need a well-documented strategy to add guaranteed lifetime income annuity. The balance of Bucket 1 consists of short-term investments to be spent down over a period of 5-7 years.

Bucket one is best broken down into 2 categories. 1A will deal with a lifetime income and 1B will deal with short-term fixed income.

Bucket 1A provides income for a lifetime and the only way to guarantee a lifetime income is through an annuity. You can begin by annuitizing enough of your assets so that you can provide a 100% of your minimum acceptable level of retirement. Income annuities can provide a secure income for an entire lifetime of 25 to 40 percent less money than it would cost you to build your own level of lifetime income. To calculate how much is needed to annuitize, you subtract the amount you'll be getting from social security and any other pension benefits from the amount you'll need each month.

Bucket 1B deals with short-term, safe and non-volatile investments that will generate income. It provides money to be spent roughly over a five-year period. An example is cash deposits offered by banks and brokerages that pay a fixed rate of interest for a prescribed period. With CDs, there's a guarantee of recovering your principal plus the additional interest on the investment.

Government bond funds are mutual funds that invest in debt instruments issued by the U.S. government and its various agencies. Treasury bills and treasury bonds are examples of government bond funds. This is a good choice for retirees looking for a low-risk supplementary income source. Floating rate funds are a higher-yielding alternative for bucket 1B. These funds contain securities with a variable interest or dividend rate.

Bucket 2 (Relative Safety)

This is a midpoint between bucket 1 and 3. The investments in Bucket 3 are only slightly more aggressive than those of Bucket 1. This bucket contains investments such as midterm bonds, mortgage-backed securities, and perhaps corporate and high yield bonds. The trick here is upon depletion of your bucket 1; you empty bucket 2 into it for another specified number of years. Bucket 3, which is a long-term investment bucket reserved for real estate, stocks, and alternative investments, is left and continues to grow. To remain consistent with the science of these buckets, it's best not to tamper too much with bucket 2.

Fixed annuities are one of the assets that I am placing in this bucket. You can get this from life insurance companies that declare and of course guarantee a certain interest rate. Just like other retirement accounts, fixed annuities also carry the tax penalty on withdrawals before 59, and a half of 10 percent federal tax and possible state tax too.

Corporate bonds or Corporate bond funds also make up bucket 2. These are debts instruments issued by a corporation and are usually long-term. Generally, corporate bond funds have a maturity period of at least a year after the date they are issued. The returns you will get from a corporate bond fund are significantly higher than a government fund, but they come with a greater risk. One major risk associated with corporate bond funds is that when the corporation goes bankrupt, there is a huge potential for a loss.

Your bucket 2 should also contain high yield bond funds which are mutual funds that invest in junk bonds. These bonds have a very low rating and highly risky. The reason for this increased risk can be easily traced to the corporations that issue the bond. These corporations are usually new ones with no proven track record of sales and earnings. They could also be corporations facing financial difficulties or ones with history of financial difficulties. These factors combine to increase the risk of their bonds, but with a potential for a high yield.

International bond funds are mutual bond funds that invest primarily in foreign debt instruments. You can purchase foreign bonds throughout the world or limit your investments to a few countries. This shouldn't be confused with a global bond fund, however, which invests in both U.S. markets and overseas markets. It is a very profitable idea for anyone planning for their retirement to add an international bond fund to their portfolio to hedge against the U.S. bond funds and the weakening dollar.

Other investments that could be added to your bucket 2 are the fixed income annuities, the principal protected annuities and the Ginnie Mae bond funds. The Ginnie Mae funds contain government-backed securities and are usually safer. These bonds are backed by the "full faith and credit" of the government and guarantee monthly payments to its investors.

Bucket 3 (Growth)

The long-term investments are in bucket 3. These are investments created and designed to be left untouched for extended periods of time. This part of your portfolio will account for actual growth. You will need for more income in the coming years after your retirement. Bucket 3 ensures that those needs are adequately tended to.

Just as it is with buckets 1, we can also split bucket 3 into sub-buckets.

Bucket 3A deals with growth and income. The focus of this bucket is the growth of your portfolio with a great emphasis on high-dividend-yielding investments. There are several ways you can achieve this growth such as: buying high dividend stocks, preferred stocks, closed-end funds, unit investments trusts, royalty trusts, and real estate investment trusts (REITs), particularly non-traded.

REITs are companies that own and operate real estates that produce rent. They own any type of real estate that generates income. These include apartment buildings, shopping centers, office towers, hotels, warehouses, golf courses, you name it. Typically, REITs collect money from you –the investor – to buy and control any type of these real estate properties that produce income in the form of rent. This rent is then divided amongst investors in the form of dividends. The beauty of a REIT for you as an investor is the safety and simplicity it offers your portfolio. A REIT is simple, less risky, and more diversified than buying the property yourself. REITs are also inflation-proof. Your REITs increase with inflation so the dividends you receive can offer protection during periods of rising prices.

The REITs we've discussed here are exclusively nontraded. Traded REITs also exist and have fundamental differences in comparison to their non-traded counterparts. As their name implies, traded REITs are traded on the stock exchange, and their prices fluctuate with the conditions of the market. Nontraded REITs don't trade on the exchange and are immune to the ravaging daily fluctuations that come with the stock market.

Bucket 3B is the long-term growth category. I'd like to place a little emphasis on value-averaging here. There is always a possibility that you exceed your investment targets in some quarters or fall below your expectations in other places. Value-averaging involves selling securities in places that have performed beyond expectations and using that income to replenish the buckets that have dropped below your target figures. This ensures that a balance is maintained throughout your investment buckets. Sub bucket 3B also allows you to consider other very profitable and long-term investments such as oil and gas master limited partnerships, private equity arrangements, royalty income trusts, and commodities.

Annuities Quiz

Before we proceed to the next chapter, I have created a checklist for you to help decide if life annuities are right for you. You will find below eight questions that will assist you in making your decision. Cfircle the appropriate answer to each question. Upon completion of the checklist, if you have 25 or more points, then annuities are the way to go for you.

Do you or your spouse expect to live beyond the age of 90

   5 points: Yes

   0 points: No

Are you a conservative investor?

   5 points: Yes

   3 points: Moderate

   1 point: Aggressive

As far as leaving your children an inheritance, you believe:

   5 points: If they get anything that's great, but not at the expense of your current lifestyle

3 points: You would like to leave them something, but it is not a top priority

1 point: You want to leave them the maximum amount

What kind of investor do you consider yourself?

5 points: Novice

3 points: Average

1 point: Excellent

Your pensions and social security income represent...

5 points: Less than 25% of your retirement income need

3 points: Less than 50% of your retirement income need

1 point: More than 50% of your retirement income need

You want to take a distribution of...

5 points: More than 4% from your investment portfolio

3 points: 4% or less from your investment portfolio

1 point: You don't need to take anything at retirement

How old are you?

5 points: Over 59.5

3 points: Between 50 and 59.5

1 point: Under 50

You believe the stock market will produce returns of

5 points: 8 percent

3 points: 6-8 percent

1 point: Less than 6 percent

What was your score? If you scored below 18 points annuities are not likely the right choice for you. A score of 18 – 24 points means you should be wary when considering annuities. Speak to an advisor about your situation. Did you score above 25? You are a strong candidate. Annuities should be a good option for you.

Chapter 4: Preparing for Whatever the Future Holds

You have entered the stage in your life where your greatest concern financially is centered on how you retire. A good retirement plan helps you prepare for whatever the future holds. In preparation for the uncertainties of the future, you must take steps and precautions that ensure that you're ready for anything. You must rebuild and increase your savings by trimming your debts and your budget while continuing to save for retirement. You should also guard your money and savings against inflation.

Planning for the future means making sacrifices in the present. These sacrifices will help you save money and will be well worth it in the end. One way to save money, for example, would be determining which frivolous expenses can be cut. A daily latte or frequent take out can be replaced by making your coffee at home or grocery shopping responsibly. Think about where your dollars go, even if it's just a regular small expenditure. It can add up. In a short time, you will be surprised at how much money you have saved putting this into practice.

Saving and cutting costs, while helpful, cannot be your only solution. You must find ways to generate additional income. This is where this book comes in. Proper investing can be the solution to getting you on the right track to your dream retirement.

With investing you will analyze many things including the stock market, and suddenly you become very interested in fluctuations in the value of securities. But you must not neglect another aspect of your life that requires careful analysis, yourself. You must consider many things; your current job, your annual income, and your state of health when preparing a retirement plan. If there's the slightest indication that you might have a health problem or a family history of some terminal disease, increase your savings accordingly. You also want to examine your expenses and determine how much you want to save for your retirement to maintain your lifestyle.

As an investor preparing for retirement, you must assess your timeline. Your age is a very important factor to consider while making decisions about your future. If you're under 40, you are in an easier position. You have a couple of decades ahead of you to build your resources and develop your portfolio. You can save early and regularly to benefit from your investments compounding. You can make systemic investments and reinvest your dividends allowing yourself the opportunity to benefit from future bull markets.

If you're between 40-55, you want to invest more in your 401(k) while searching for other ways to stock away money.

If you're fifty-five and older, you may start getting notions of retiring early and start digging into your retirement savings. I recommend giving it a few more years and avoiding raiding into your retirement account too early. You could also plan on a possible part-time work in the earlier stages of retirement. This provides extra income to cover for what you may be spending from your retirement account. It is also important that at this stage, you take care of yourself and put your needs first.

Chapter 6: Getting to Safety in Four Amazingly Logical Steps

Determining Your Budget

Step 1: Determine Spending

The first step to consider is to find out how much you are spending now. You can do this by going through your checkbooks, bank statements and credit cards; add up what it cost you to live over the past few months. Now, subtract all the expenses related to work. You will not need to consider the ones you will no longer incur when leaving your job. These often include commuting costs, office clothing, take-home dinners, subscriptions to industry websites and publications, dues to professional clubs, contribution to retirement plans, social security, and health insurance. If you have credit card debt, include the cost of an accelerated repayment plan. You will also want to add what it costs to buy Medicare or a private health insurance plan.

Step 2: List all salary-type income you expect or are receiving as a retiree

This list will include things such as social security, pensions, rental income, any royalties, trust income and so on. Do not include any income from interest and dividends. You must consider what income you will have prior to your investment strategy. This will help you determine how much you need to make up the difference based on what you calculated in Step 1.

Step 3: Add up the current value of all your financial assets

These financial assets include savings, retirement accounts, mutual funds, stocks, and bonds. After getting the current value of all your assets, assume that you are going to spend 4% of the sum on annually on your living expenses.

Step 4: Let's do the math!

Add the 4% from your financial assets to your total salary-type income and subtract an estimate from income taxes. The remainder is roughly the amount you can safely spend each year without running out of money.

Please note that married couples should do this retirement calculation in three ways; as a couple; and once for each partner if the other dies.

Budget Process Considerations:

Seven situations should be considered in the budget process;

Real Estate

There are multiple ways you can use your home equity to close a gap between your retirement income and expenses. You can sell your house, add the proceeds to your investments and rent an apartment. You can also sell the house, buy something cheaper and put the remaining money into investments or cash reserves. This equity plan comes into play when your current finances don't meet your expectation.

Health Care

People on Medicare often spend a lot of money due to routine visits to the doctor. You could be spending an average of two thousand dollars a year on hospital visits. The cost may be higher for people with high-deductible health insurance plans as well as patients with chronic illness. You can save and prepare these situations by deciding to spend a little less than 4 percent of your retirement reserve.

Debt

Debt can cripple retirees. If you are still working and in the retirement planning stage, try to clear your debts as this will help your savings last longer.

Caretaking

If you are working and your spouse falls seriously ill, it's advisable to hire some health personnel rather than quit your job and become their personal care-taker. This way you could still get regular income to support their care many other needs. Take this cost into consideration if it may arise during your retirement.

Helping your children

Your money is entirely yours, and you are not obligated to give any to your kids. You have fulfilled your duty in raising them and giving them the life you could afford. Their standard of living from here lies in their own hands. Whatever you decide to give them should be at your discretion and perhaps because they deserve it and not out of an obligation to do so.

Special Purchases

Money meant for special purchases such as a new car, vacation, and home additions should be set aside in a bank account for such purposes. Your savings should cover large cash expenses that you can predict.

An Inheritance

If you are expecting an inheritance, the best advice is to plan your budget without the inheritance. Let your budget be based on your own resources.

If you hire a financial planner to help, ensure that he or she is duty bound to put your financial interests ahead of theirs. They should give you the best advice possible regardless of the amount of money you pay for their services. Either you create your retirement plan yourself or with help, assume that you will live a long and active life.

Once you follow these four steps and determine how much money you need, you'll be able to implement the rules and strategies we discussed in the beginning of the book. This should all be coming together now!

Chapter 7: How to Double Your Social Security Income

Social Security Basic Benefits

Primary Insurance Amount (PIA): This is the monthly benefit you will receive if you retire at your full retirement age. It is the most important number in your social security record. Early retirement benefits are a discount from your PIA. If your pay goes up, your PIA goes up. The inverse is also true, if your pay goes down, your PIA reduces. If you keep working on starting your benefits, social security will add those earnings to your record.

Cost-of-living-adjustment (COLA): When you are on social security, you get a cost-of-living increase every year when inflation is 0.1 percent or more. With this, your purchasing power is secure no matter how high the inflation flies. Most states and private pensions provide a fixed income that suffers a loss in purchasing power every year.

Along with the benefits you receive, special benefits go to your spouse if they lack a sufficient social security account of their own. Ex-spouses can also make a claim on your account provided that the marriage lasted at least ten years.

In addition to spousal benefits, there are four benefits that are available to your family if you die. They include:

- Survivor's benefits for your spouse (and qualified ex-spouse)
- Parental benefits for a spouse (or ex-spouse) who is taking care of your child who is under 16 years old or disabled (the disability must have started before the child reached 22 years)
- Benefits for your children if they are under 18 (or 19 and attending high school)
- Parental benefits if you have been paying more than half the support for an aging parent

All these payments, however, receive cost-of-living increases. Any money owed to you will be paid to you subsequently.

Note that only your earnings and wages from self-employment count toward your earnings limit. Social security looks only at what you personally bring in. The earnings limit for 2016 was

$15,760 from ages below 65 years and $41,880 in the year you are 66. The Government worker test affects people with government pensions who also worked at least ten years in the private sector.

Your social security statement shows your future estimated social security payment at various ages as well as benefits for your family. Retirement benefits are monthly checks you are entitled to receive based on your personal earnings record. If you worked fewer than 35 years, you get nothing for each missing year.

Your full retirement age is a magic number because this is the age you claim your PIA. Early retirement has its disadvantages as it reduces your benefits. As much as 25% could be deducted from the benefits. You can also decide to put your checks on hold in case you don't want to take your benefits early. Just do well to inform social security.

What You Need to Know about Collecting Benefits

Spousal Benefits

As a spouse, you can claim benefits based on the earning records of your husband or wife. You get up to half of the primary insurance that your partner is entitled to at full retirement age. However, to receive such benefits, your mate must be at least 62 years old and must have claimed the benefits. If your spouse delays his or her claim, your spousal benefits will also be delayed. For a full spousal benefit, you must reach your full retirement age.

You cannot receive retirement benefits on your own account and afterwards switch to the spousal benefit. This is because when you apply for a social security claim, you are deemed to be applying for both at once. If you are married and the both of you are 66 years old, you can't both claim spousal benefits on the other's account.

Information for Divorced Spouses

A marriage which spanned for at least ten years without remarriage will qualify for spousal and survivor benefits based on your ex's earnings record.

There are seven rules I'd like to cover:

1. Vexations should not lead to divorce if the marriage is close to ten years. In severe cases, save the marriage through an informal separation until the time is up.
2. You must wait until you are 66 years old for spousal benefits even if you're caring for a child.
3. You can claim spousal benefit if your spouse has not filed for retirement once your ex is eligible and has been divorced for two years or more.
4. Remarriage will make you claim benefits on the current spouse. And if it lasts for ten years before a divorce, you can claim benefit on either based on the higher benefit.

5. In the event of their death, you'll get a survivor's benefit if you're not remarried and the marriage lasted for ten years. If you remarried, you can get benefits on the new spouse if you're sixty and above and the marriage lasted ten years at least.
6. You don't have to be in contact with your ex-spouse before you claim your benefit, but your divorce decree is needed.
7. Payments made to a divorced spouse or two exes do not reduce benefits for a worker or current spouse.

Decision Time: Needs from Social Security

Your personal goals will determine your path.

Is your goal immediate cash? This will result in more spending money temporarily but over time, it will reduce. To achieve the largest possible monthly benefit, claim it at seventy. If married, a dependent spouse gets the highest survivor's benefit. To maximize the benefits as a couple throughout your life, either should begin retirement benefits at sixty or sixty-six no matter the cost.

If you're divorced and you're healthy, start benefits shortly before or at seventy. Each year you delay retirement after your full retirement age, your benefit on primary insurance grows by eight percent. Begin benefits at sixty-six if you're sixty and believe you may die before your average life expectancy. This should be based on a personal medical condition. Also, sixty-six can be chosen if that is the only option for payment of bills.

Special note for an older, single parent with a young child: If a child is eighteen (or nineteen if still in high school) benefits on retired parent's social security can be received if there is a retirement claim by the parent. The child may be biological, adopted, or even stepchild.

Getting The Most from Social Security When Married

If the breadwinner dies first and there is an early filing, survivor benefit will reduce. If your goal is to maximize your income as a one-earner couple, you should consider this:

If you are of the same age, the breadwinner and dependent spouse should file at full retirement age (66 or 67). In this case, you're eligible for full spousal benefit without a discount. If the breadwinner is slightly older, the breadwinner should file at full retirement age. Where the breadwinner is four years older or more, the breadwinner should wait until seventy then file at full retirement age to claim the highest survivor benefit.

Everything changes if both spouses have decent earning records meaning neither will get the spousal benefit but will receive a retirement benefit higher than the spousal benefit. This will also be based on your personal account. The filing time will be based on how much increment you want for future benefits. Income maximization will occur if you both live long as a couple and claim at age seventy, even though it is not the best. It's better for the lower-earning spouse to file for a reduced benefit at 66 while the higher waits until 70.

Born in 1953 or Earlier

Take advantage of what others can't gain because only you can collect spousal and retirement benefit. People qualified are two-earner couples, each having substantial social security account. This can succeed in either way:

The first, the lower-earning spouse claims reduced retirement benefits at 66. When the higher earner is 66, they put in a restricted application for spousal benefits on the lower-earning spouse's account. The higher earner collects the benefits for four years. At seventy, they switch to the higher earner's retirement account. Alternatively, the older of the couple files for retirement benefits when the younger reaches full retirement age. Specify to social security that you are filing for a spousal benefit only. Eligibility involves filing at the right age, if you were born in 1953 or earlier, and you are eligible.

As a widow or widower, if your spouse died early and you have a job, it is advisable to file for survivor's benefit. Also, if a spouse has been collecting the benefit of the other who is dead, the spousal benefits will step up. To get the most from social security when divorced, two things are involved. The first is the size of your social security earnings record compared with that of your ex. The second is your age when you make your claim. If you have no retirement benefit of your own, you will depend on what you receive as an ex-spouse, usually 30 to 35 percent check reduction if you file at 66. Also, waiting to file for full retirement at 66 or 67 will result in your spouse's benefit and half of the ex's primary insurance.

If you are still working, put up a claim at full retirement at 66 or 67 to avoid reaching earning limits. If you were born in 1953 or earlier, at 70, you can switch to your personal benefits that would have been enhanced by eight percent.

If your ex-spouse dies and you haven't remarried, you get one hundred percent of what your ex received if you file at the full retirement age, and you also get survivor's benefits. If you lay an early claim to it, it reduces.

If your ex-spouse files for retirement benefits and suspends it voluntarily, you won't be able to collect on his or her account. Getting the most from social security as a family involves your family getting social security on your record if you filed for retirement, become disabled, or die.

Getting the Most Out of Social Security as a Family

The area of coverage here includes natural and adopted children, stepchildren, and children in the care of an ex-spouse. In some special cases, it also covers grandchildren who are dependents. Children with serious disabilities continue to receive benefits after they turn 18, but this is conditional on the fact that the disability struck before the child was 2 years old. The mother's or father's benefits go to the surviving spouse taking care of the child. The spouse shouldn't be married, and their wages should be below the earning limit, else the check would be reduced. Ex-spouses would only be considered if they are unmarried and caring for the worker's adopted or natural child.

Aging parents also get benefits if the worker who dies has been paying more than half of their benefits. But the earning shouldn't be more than their social security payments. The amount to be paid to the family is limited and it must not be exceeded. You can handle family benefits by opening a retirement benefit account, so your spouse and children can claim your account. On the account of a deceased spouse, you can file for a father or mother's benefit. With young children, it further solidifies your claim even if your pay is above the social security limit. Claiming benefits as a young parent will not infringe on you claiming the spouse benefits at an older age. Children benefit payments run for up to six months but will extend to 12 months if the child is disabled. If you file for benefits after you retire, social security will backtrack your application and pay for some of the missing months.

If you claimed benefits too early and then regret it, there are two ways you can remedy that. You can either carry out a do-over or opt for voluntary suspension. Do-over is about you withdrawing your claim with social security. It can only be done if you change your mind within the first 12 months of starting the retirement benefits payment. You then file for withdrawal of claims with social security and pay back the money you have already received, and you begin anew. But this can only be done once, so make it count. If 12 months have passed, then you are no longer eligible for a do-over. You can ask social security to suspend your current benefits, but this is only possible if you have attained the full retirement age of 66 or 67. The payment is then stopped, and no money must be returned. But there is a note of warning to this, and that is voluntary suspension also stops the payment of claims to others. Spouses, ex-spouses and qualified children can't be paid until you continue receiving your benefits.

CASH-RICH RETIREMENT

A solid step in securing a cash-rich retirement is saving at least 20% of your pre-tax income. In your 20's you should save 10-15% of your salary. In your 30's 15-25%, your early 40's 25-35% should be put aside as savings.

There are 6 steps to follows to make your retirement plan bulletproof.

The first is to change your "auto pilot." Second, you should diversify your investments in different ways. Third, you need to build a viable investment plan. Fourth is to get as much professional help as you can. Fifth, build income streams via a ladder of annuities. Lastly, invest in health care insurance.

You must learn how to save. You need to go from that guy who says, "I can't save" to the guy who says, "I save automatically!" To be able to save, you should itemize your expenditure for the last 6 months, then set a plan and cut 5% of your monthly expenditure and divert the sum into your savings. You should also read books on savings and apply the suggested techniques. You can also automatically deduct part of your pay and contribute to your company's 401(k) or any other savings platform.

Give your broker information on what strategy to use. Make sure that any returns you make are automatically reinvested. Also, you should also try to be dynamic with your investment. As the market changes flow with the tide. There are some action steps you will implement to aid your progress. First, you should identify the income target you aspire for. Second, you should contact social security for your updated benefit statement. Third, meet other employees and find out pension qualifications. Fourth, you should find out the present saving requirements, how much you have, and how much is needed. Fifth, set yourself a disciplined savings plan and make sure you can stick to it. Finally set your sights on hard income for investments and follow the golden rule which is; don't speculate.

INVESTMENT MASTER PLAN

There are some investment blueprints that should guide you in choosing what and what to plunge your money into. For interest incomes, you can make up to 20% interest in the U.S. and 5% outside. Short maturity bank deposit, bond funds, Treasury Inflation Protection (TIN) fund, and International bond funds all amount to interest income. Also, there is the Dividend Income where you can make up to 25% interest in both the U.S. and outside. U.S. stock index, low and high earning stock, international stock, emerging and actively managed stock funds all unite to form dividend income. You can also make 5% interest from the U.S. and 10% outside the U.S. through Rent Income. U.S. nonresidential and international real estate fund help actualize this. While for Insurance Investments 10% profit is attainable outside the U.S. while in the U.S. the odds are bleak. All these portfolios add up to 50% interest in the U.S. and another 50 in non-U.S.

BUILDING INCOME STREAMS WITH A LADDER OF ANNUITIES

The type of annuity you choose specifies the number of years you will be paid. An individual payout is the type of annuity that pays you for the rest of your life. The joint survivor annuity keeps paying till the death of you and your spouse or the designated beneficiary. While the joint life annuity keeps paying until the death of either you or your spouse. When buying an annuity choose one with contract terms that are easy to understand. You should go for a single life annuity if single, and the joint survivorship if in a relationship. If you die before you begin receiving payments, your heir will receive the sum of the premium paid or the value of the investment and this is called Death Benefit.

There are some things that you should consider before choosing an annuity. Avoid annuities with high sale commission, administrative expenses, long penalty periods and so on. Try to spread it and buy different annuities that will pay you different amounts at different periods. Try to go for fund managers offering you multiple tools of international funds. They should also be able to offer dividends oriented equity funds. Some annuities also allow you to invest money in an account and get a 12 or 24-month return. But this feature can only be gotten from reputable insurance companies with the financial wherewithal.

A LIFE CYCLE ANNUITY STRATEGY

Take active control of your income with different annuity forms. Annuity 1 covers your income for nine years (65-74 years), Annuity 2 covers you for another nine years (75-84 years) and Annuity 3 covers your income for life (85-life). Annuity 1 offers you more payments till you retire at age 67, Annuity 2 gives you more monthly payments till you retire and Annuity 3 is a deferred variable bought that can be converted to a fixed annuity later.

You can invest into annuities by buying a diversified mix of American and International income-oriented bonds, real estate and equity. Annually guaranteed returns and equity funds are means of investing in Annuity 2. While investments in Annuity 3 are done more conservatively through stocks, guaranteed funds and so on. Annuity 3 gives you a fixed return from that time with a longevity coverage.

CONCLUSION

In the end, what the future holds is entirely in your hands. What I hope to have achieved with this book hopefully to assist you in ensuring the future that is on the horizon is one that has been properly planned. It is my hope that you take advantage of the well-researched strategies this book offers and secure your retiring years.

You can gather a lot more information on the internet about the stock market. Consider all the different securities discussed this book and help yourself decide that which suits your personality best. Are you an aggressive investor or the type that leans more on the side of caution? If you don't already know this, you must ask yourself immediately. After you have decided where you fall, you need to get a financial adviser or registered investment agent(RIA) who can serve as your guide through this seemingly daunting world of stocks, bonds, and trusts.

It is important to stress that investing is far from a one size fits all. What works for Jane across the street may not really work for you. It is possible Jane has different goals from yours, and hence the strategies that work for her may not be suited for you. Find what works for you and stick to it.

Reaching your goals will take a while, could be years, but with patience, passion, and dedication, you will achieve your goals. If you have read and completely understood the guide provided here, then you are on the right path for your dream retirement.

www.ingramcontent.com/pod-product-compliance
Lightning Source LLC
Chambersburg PA
CBHW071151220526
45468CB00003B/1021